BEYOND
THE
Veil
COMPANION JOURNAL

BEYOND THE VEIL COMPANION JOURNAL

© 2023 Yvonne Allen. All Rights Reserved.

Published by Yvonne Allen | Southlake, Texas

ISBN (Print): 979-8-9889023-5-5

Printed in the United States of America

Prepared for Publication: www.wendykwalters.com

Cover Photo: Abrahanny Rodriguez | www.abrahanny.com

To contact the author:
YVONNEALLEN.COM

You are Invited

I created this companion journal for you to use as you read through *Beyond the Veil*. Along the way there are some scriptures and questions to prompt you. I invite you to journal with the Bridegroom King as He speaks to your heart and beckons you to draw near to Him.

Yvonne Allen
Beyond the Veil

Let us rejoice and exalt Him
and give Him glory, because
the wedding celebration
of the Lamb has come.
And His bride has
made herself ready.
Fine linen, shining bright
and clear, has been given to
her to wear, and the fine linen
represents the righteous
deeds of His holy believers.

REVELATION 19:7-8, TPT

SUBJECT   PAGE #

Awake, you who sleep,
Arise from the dead,
and Christ will give you light.

THE BRIDEGROOM KING
EPHESIANS 5:14, NKJV

Arise, my dearest.

Hurry, my darling.

Come away with me!

I have come as you have asked

to draw you to my heart

and lead you out.

For now is the time, my beautiful one.

THE BRIDEGROOM KING

SONG OF SONGS 2:10, TPT

The season has changed,
the bondage of your
barren winter has ended,
and the season of hiding
is over and gone.
The rains have soaked the earth...

THE BRIDEGROOM KING

SONG OF SONGS 2:11, TPT

... and left it bright with blossoming flowers. The season for singing and pruning the vines has arrived. I hear the cooing of doves in our land, filling the air with songs to awaken you and guide you forth.

THE BRIDEGROOM KING

SONG OF SONGS 2:12, TPT

Can you not discern this new day of
destiny breaking forth around you?
The early signs of purpose and
plans are bursting forth.
The budding vines of new life are
now blooming everywhere.
The fragrance of their flowers whispers,
"There is change in the air."
Arise, my love, my beautiful companion,
and run with me to a higher place.
For now is the time to arise
and come away with me.

THE BRIDEGROOM KING

SONG OF SONGS 2:13, TPT

For you are my dove, hidden
in the split-open rock.
It was I who took you and hid you up
high in the secret stairway of the sky.
Let me see your radiant face
and hear your sweet voice.
How beautiful your eyes of worship
and lovely your voice in prayer.

THE BRIDEGROOM KING

SONG OF SONGS 2:14, TPT

Do you operate in pride or surrender?

Are you a faithful, loving servant in God's house?

How does this manifest in your life?

In what lovely or unexpected ways
has Father shown up for you?

How do daughters think differently
than servants or friends?

When you have moments of extreme faith followed by moments of extreme doubt, what do you do?

How do the responsibilities and privileges
of being a bride differ from being a daughter?

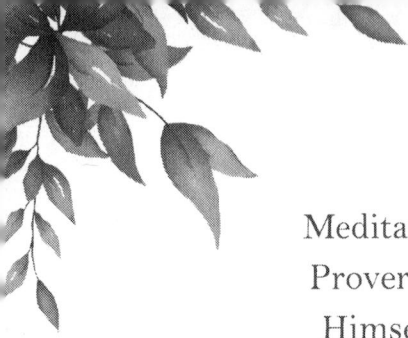

Meditate on this list of things from
Proverbs 31 and ask God to reveal
Himself to you as your Husband,
and you as His bride.

1. I am *more precious* than *jewels*—valuable and rare.

2. My Husband *trusts* me—I do him good and not evil.

3. I am *industrious*—willing to serve.

4. I *take care* of His estate—procure what is
   needed, and manage His household.

5. I am *prosperous*—I buy and sell for a profit.

6. I am *strong*—there is nothing feeble about me.

7. I am *generous*—I notice and give to the poor.

8. I *rejoice*—I am clothed in strength and honor.

9. I am *wise*—I give sound counsel, and I am kind.

10. I am *watchful*—aware of myself
    and those in my charge.

11. I am *worthy of praise*—my children and my
    Husband bless me; my works bear witness.

12. I *fear the Lord*—I approach Him with holy
    reverence, and I am in awe of His power,
    majesty, goodness, grace, mercy, and love.

In what ways are you walking toward Jesus (as His bride)?
In what ways is the Holy Spirit walking by your side?

Have you ever dealt with an orphan spirit?

Explain why or why not.

You must catch the troubling foxes,
those sly little foxes that
hinder our relationship.
For they raid our
budding vineyard of love
to ruin what
I've planted within you.
Will you catch them and
remove them for me?
We will do it together.

THE BRIDEGROOM KING

SONG OF SONGS 2:15, TPT

O my beloved, you are lovely.

When I see you in your beauty,

I see a radiant city where

we will dwell as one.

More pleasing than any pleasure,

more delightful than any delight,

you have ravished my heart,

stealing away my strength to resist you.

Even hosts of angels stand in awe of you.

THE BRIDEGROOM KING

SONG OF SONGS 6:4, TPT

The shining of your spirit
shows how you have taken my truth
to become balanced and complete.

THE BRIDEGROOM KING

SONG OF SONGS 6:6, TPT

But unique is my beloved dove—

unrivaled in beauty,

without equal, beyond compare,

the perfect one, the favorite one.

Others see your beauty

and sing of your joy.

Brides and queens chant your praise:

"How blessed is she!"

THE BRIDEGROOM KING

SONG OF SONGS 6:9, TPT

How beautiful on the mountains
are the sandaled feet of this one
bringing such good news.
You are truly royalty!
The way you walk so gracefully
in my ways displays such dignity.
You are truly the poetry of
God—His very handiwork.

THE BRIDEGROOM KING

SONG OF SONGS 7:1, TPT

Made in the USA
Las Vegas, NV
01 October 2023

78383878R00072